CountryMusic ★ Stars
TAYLOR SWIFT

By Mary Molly Shea

Gareth Stevens

Please visit our Web site www.garethstevens.com. For a free color catalog of all our high-quality books, call toll free 1-800-542-2595 or fax 1-877-542-2596.

Library of Congress Cataloging-in-Publication Data

Shea, Mary Molly.
Taylor Swift / Mary Molly Shea.
    p. cm. — (Country music stars)
Includes index.
ISBN 978-1-4339-3611-1 (pbk.)
ISBN 978-1-4339-3612-8 (6-pack)
ISBN 978-1-4339-3610-4 (library binding)
1. Swift, Taylor, 1989—Juvenile literature. 2. Women country musicians—United States—Biography—Juvenile literature. I. Title.
ML3930.S989S54 2010
782.421642092—dc22
[B]

2009040600

Published in 2010 by Gareth Stevens Publishing
111 East 14th Street, Suite 349
New York, NY 10003

Designer: Michael J. Flynn
Editor: Therese Shea

Photo credits: Cover (background) Shutterstock.com; cover (Taylor Swift), pp. 1, 23 © Jason Kempin/Getty Images; p. 5 © Rick Diamond/Getty Images; p. 7 © A. Messerschmidt/Getty Images; p. 9 © Scott Gries/Getty Images; p. 11 © Kevin Winter/Getty Images; pp. 13, 29 © Ethan Miller/Getty Images; p. 15 © Theo Wargo/WireImage/Getty Images; p. 17 © Rick Diamond/WireImage/ Getty Images; p. 19 © Frazer Harrison/ACM2009/Getty Images; p. 21 © Alberto E. Rodriguez/Getty Images; p. 25 © Frank Micelotta/Getty Images; p. 27 © Shirlaine Forrest/WireImage/Getty Images.

Printed in the United States of America

CPSIA compliance information: Batch #CW10GS: For further information contact Gareth Stevens, New York, New York at 1-800-542-2595.

CONTENTS

It's Taylor!   4

Young Singer   6

Writing Songs   10

Taylor's Albums   14

All About Taylor   20

Taylor's Songs   26

Timeline   30

For More Information   31

Glossary   32

Index   32

IT'S TAYLOR!

Taylor Swift is a country music singer.

She composes many of her own songs.

YOUNG SINGER

Taylor was born in Wyomissing, Pennsylvania, in 1989. She sang at fairs when she was very young.

Taylor recorded herself singing.

She gave her recorded songs to

music companies.

WRITING SONGS

Taylor learned to play the guitar when she was 12. She began to compose her own music.

When she was 14, Taylor moved near Nashville, Tennessee. She got a job composing songs.

13

TAYLOR'S ALBUMS

A recording company asked Taylor to make an album. It came out in 2006. It was a hit!

Taylor wrote a song called "Tim McGraw." In 2007, she went on tour with Tim McGraw and Faith Hill!

Tim
McGraw

Faith
Hill

17

Taylor made another album called *Fearless.* It was named Album of the Year in 2009!

FEARLESS

Taylor Swift

ALL ABOUT TAYLOR

Taylor has famous friends, such as Miley Cyrus. Sometimes, Taylor and Miley sing together!

Miley
Cyrus

21

Some of Taylor's songs tell a story.

Sometimes, she sings in a costume.

Taylor loves her fans. She takes time to talk with them.

TAYLOR'S SONGS

Taylor sings about love. She sings about her life.

In 2009, Taylor became the youngest person to ever be named Entertainer of the Year. She will be singing for years to come!

TIMELINE

1989   Taylor Swift is born in Wyomissing, Pennsylvania.

2002   Taylor learns to play the guitar.

2004   Taylor moves near Nashville, Tennessee.

2006   Taylor's first album comes out.

2007   Taylor goes on tour with Tim McGraw and Faith Hill.

2009   Taylor's second album is named Album of the Year.

2009   Taylor is named Entertainer of the Year.

FOR MORE INFORMATION

Books:

Parvis, Sarah. *Taylor Swift*. Kansas City, MO:
Andrews McMeel Publishing, 2009.

Rawson, Katherine. *Taylor Swift*. New York:
Rosen Publishing, 2009.

Reusser, Kayleen. *Taylor Swift*. Hockessin, DE:
Mitchell Lane Publishers, 2009.

Web Sites:

Big Machine Records: Taylor Swift

www.bigmachinerecords.com/taylorswift/

Taylor Swift: Official Site

www.taylorswift.com

GLOSSARY

compose: to write a piece of music

costume: clothes that make a person look like someone or something else

entertainer: person who acts, sings, dances, or plays music for others

record: to make a copy of sounds

tour: a trip to many places in order to entertain people

INDEX

album 14, 18, 30
Album of the Year 18, 30
compose 4, 10, 12
costume 22
Cyrus, Miley 20
fairs 6
Fearless 18

guitar 10, 30
Hill, Faith 16, 30
McGraw, Tim 16, 30
Nashville, Tennessee 12, 30
record 8, 14

"Tim McGraw" 16
Wyomissing, Pennsylvania 6, 30